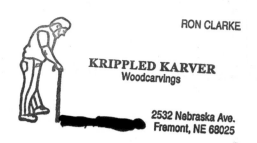

MW00637283

# Carving Classic Swan and Goose Decoys

Ready-to-Use Templates for Making Reproductions
of 16 Antique Carvings

ANTHONY HILLMAN

DOVER PUBLICATIONS, INC., NEW YORK

*To Bill and Muriel Tullner*
*"Good friends calm the roughest seas."*

The author wishes to acknowledge with thanks the help of the following: Jim and Joan Siebert, Bill and Muriel Tullner, Jamie Hand, John Steed, Arlene Saunders, and John and Isabelle Hillman.

Copyright © 1987 by Anthony Hillman.
All rights reserved under Pan American and
International Copyright Conventions.

Published in Canada by General Publishing Company, Ltd.,
30 Lesmill Road, Don Mills, Toronto, Ontario.
Published in the United Kingdom by Constable and Company, Ltd.

*Carving Classic Swan and Goose Decoys: Ready-to-Use Templates for Making Reproductions of 16 Antique Carvings* is a new work, first published by Dover Publications, Inc., in 1987.

These patterns and drawings are not to be used for printed reproduction without permission.

Manufactured in the United States of America
Dover Publications, Inc., 31 East 2nd Street, Mineola, N.Y. 11501

*Library of Congress Cataloging-in-Publication Data*

Hillman, Anthony.
Carving classic swan and goose decoys :
ready-to-use templates for making reproductions
of 16 antique carvings / by Anthony Hillman.
p.        cm.
ISBN 0-486-25522-0 (pbk.)
1. Wood-carving—Technique.   2. Waterfowl in art.   I. Title.
NK9704.H55   1987
745.593—dc19          87-21706
CIP

# How to Carve Wooden Swans and Geese in Antique Regional Styles

The Canada Goose, one of the most widely distributed of wildfowl and long a favorite game bird, is familiar everywhere in North America. Less well known are the Whistling Swan and the Brant. This is partly because their distribution is limited and partly because decrease in numbers caused hunting of certain populations to be prohibited for many years (the swan still may not be hunted). The Whistling Swan (now named Tundra Swan; the older name is retained here because hunters and decoy carvers knew the bird by that name) is by far the more common of our two native species of swan. As it breeds in the far North of Canada and its winter range is restricted to a part of the mid-Atlantic coast and some small areas in the West, this beautiful swan is still a far from common bird, except locally. Also common only locally is the Brant, a small goose that breeds in the very far North and winters along the Pacific coast (occasionally in a few small inland localities) and on the Atlantic coast from, approximately, southern Maine to North Carolina.

The Whistling Swan and the Brant were once highly prized as game birds (the Pacific-coast race of the Brant still is), especially in the late nineteenth century. Many goose and swan decoys were created for and by hunters. Most of the swan decoys have not survived, their long necks being easily damaged. They were less common than goose and duck decoys to begin with, since a swan decoy anywhere near life-size is a bulky, cumbersome item in the cramped space of a hunter's duckboat. Most of the few swan decoys that have survived the years come from Chesapeake Bay, where large numbers of Whistling Swans still spend each winter.

Although swan decoys today are objects of interest chiefly to the collector, they are still sometimes used as "confidence" decoys. A confidence decoy is a carving of a nongame species, such as a gull, heron, or swan, that is placed among a group of decoys representing the hunted birds. The latter birds are frequently highly wary, but the apparently calm presence of other birds (sometimes normally wary themselves) tends to disarm their suspicion—gain their "confidence."

Many of the decoys in this book would be enormous if made full-size. Most hobbyists will want to make at least somewhat smaller versions; therefore the patterns, if used directly as templates, will give you the smaller-sized birds generally desirable. For those who wish to make full-size decoys, I have added data on the size of the classic original decoys on which those in this book are based. In some cases I have indicated the size of the live birds instead; this was done when accurate information on the precise size of the original carving was unobtainable.

Whatever size you intend to carve your decoys at, and for whatever purpose they are intended, you should be aware that these splendid models are the heritage of men who produced some of the finest folk sculpture ever made.

The following are a few points to keep in mind in carving your decoys. First of all, take note of the particular characteristics of the model you wish to carve. One is carved from a single piece of wood (the "Preening Brant," Plate 8). The number of separate pieces required for the others varies depending upon the style. So that the patterns can be used for purposes other than carving, and to provide a full picture of the birds, I have left the head and body patterns joined. Wherever it is indicated that the head and body are to be carved separately, separate the templates for head and body profile and use them to cut out separate pieces of wood. Also you should be aware that some decoys are hollowed out (a method preferred in some regions) while others are left solid. Study the patterns and any special instructions before you begin any work. Yet another point: while the profile patterns may always be cut out and used as templates, as well as the top view of the body in most cases (only half of this is generally given; simply flip over this piece to trace the other half onto the wood), the top and front views of the head cannot be used in this way and are intended for reference only. And finally, for each carving I have specified the *minimum-size* pieces of dressed wood required. When in doubt always use larger pieces; these of course can be readily cut down if necessary. Many types of wood suitable for carving are available locally. Obtain the best clear, straight-grained wood available in your area. And remember—always place the direction of the grain to run with the longest dimension of the piece to be carved.

Now remove the staples and spread the pages out flat. You can cut out the patterns and use them directly as templates, but I recommend that you give them permanence by gluing them to ³⁄₁₆" mahogany exterior plywood. Mahogany is recommended because even pieces as thin as these will be durable. Carefully recut the patterns. Varnish will seal the edges. Mounting the patterns in this manner will preserve them for making duplicates. On the head template, drill a hole in the eye big enough for marking eye position, if eyes are required.

Read through the following general instructions and all specific instructions for the decoy you intend to carve before taking any steps to begin carving. I will describe the method for making a hollow decoy; if the carving you are making is a solid one, simply leave out the steps for hollowing.

## The Body

For a general example, let us start with the "Shang" Wheeler Canada Goose (Plate 11). This has a body in two parts. Using the required pieces of stock, tape the two pieces of wood together with masking tape. Position the pattern so that the bottom falls right along the bottom of the wood. Mark out the profile pattern as shown in Fig. 1.

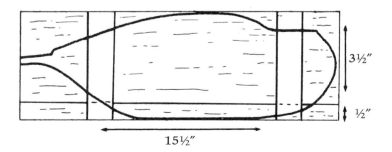

3½"

½"

15½"

*Fig. 1*

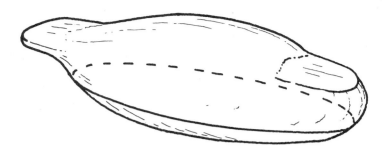

*Fig. 2*

Cut this out on a band saw, being careful to cut along the *outside* of the thick black line. Now separate the pieces, and using the top-view pattern mark each piece on the surfaces which were joined, and then bandsaw the top and bottom halves. The dashed line on the top-view pattern indicates the shape of the bottom half. Do not cut too close to the thick black lines—leave a little extra for the final shaping. Shape top and bottom halves individually, fitting the two together periodically to insure a nice rounded shape. Using a hatchet or a drawknife, cut away excess wood to get the general shape (Fig. 2). A spokeshave is used to further round and smooth the body. Leave extra surface for the neck joint.

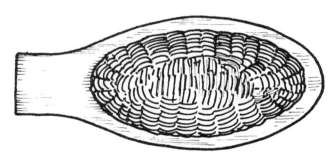

*Fig. 3*

There are several ways to hollow out a decoy body. One way is to use a 1" gouge (about a 9 sweep) and a mallet. Score the wood about ¾" from the edge to prevent splitting to the outside edge. Hollow the top section to within ½". Leave more wood in the middle of the bottom body section so you can weight it (Fig. 3). Other methods include drilling with hand drills or a drill press with Forstner bits if available. When using a drill press be sure to secure the half being drilled and to pay attention to the depth of the cut.

Note that on the "Shang" Wheeler pattern, the bottom board is not hollowed out at all. If you are using a pattern for a decoy in which the bottom part is required to be hollowed out, now is the time to hollow it. Always leave more wood in the bottom part, however; this acts as ballast in a working decoy, and

*(Instructions continue after plates.)*

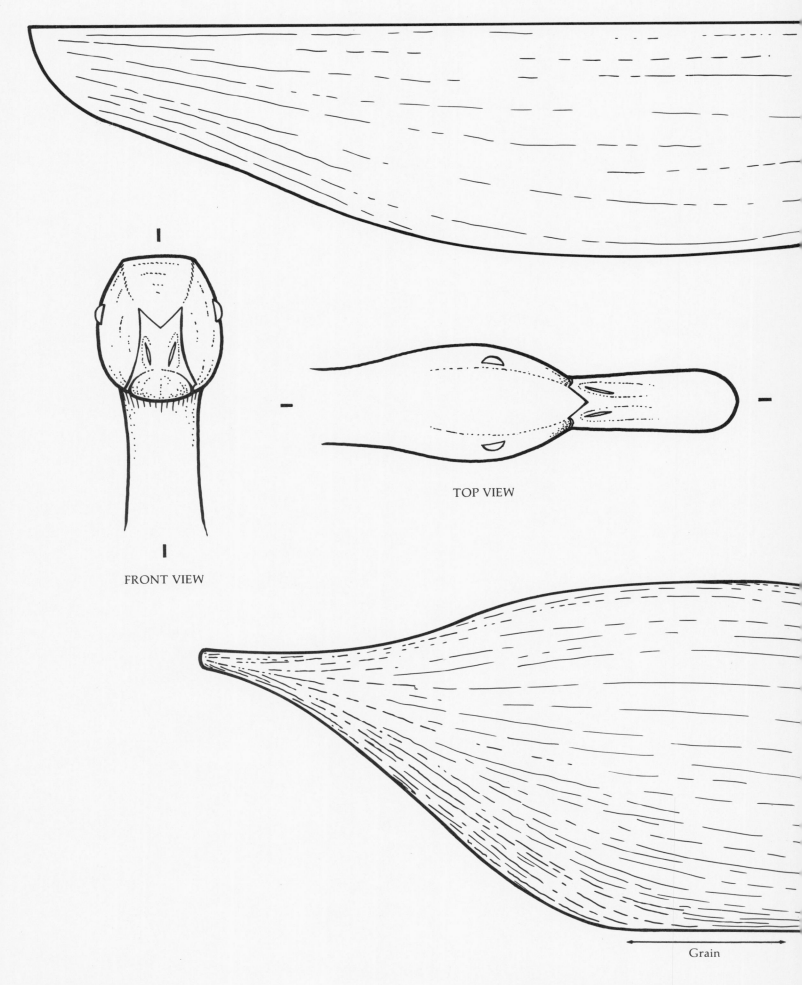

TOP VIEW

FRONT VIEW

TOP VIEW

Grain

*Plate 1 (left)*

Remove staples to see and use full patterns.

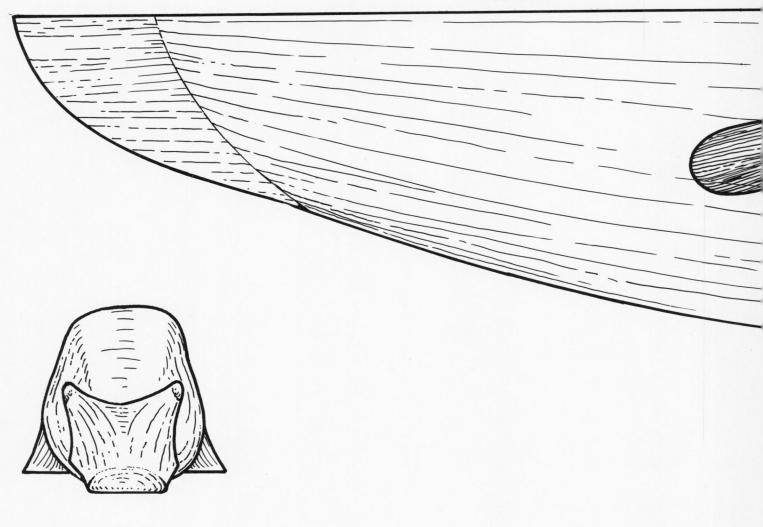

FRONT VIEW

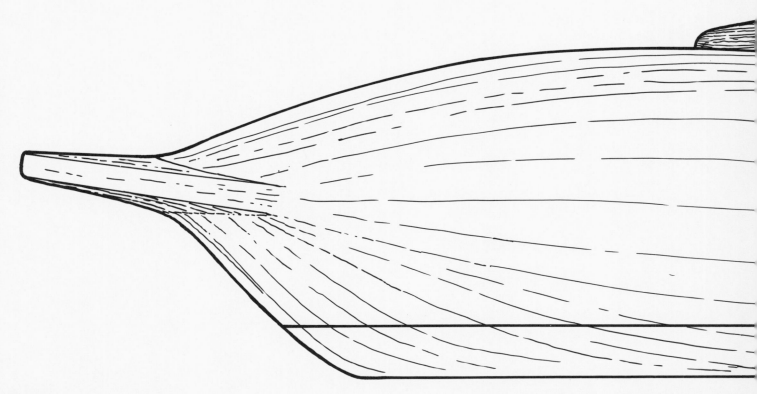

*Plate 2 (left)*

Remove staples to see and use full patterns.

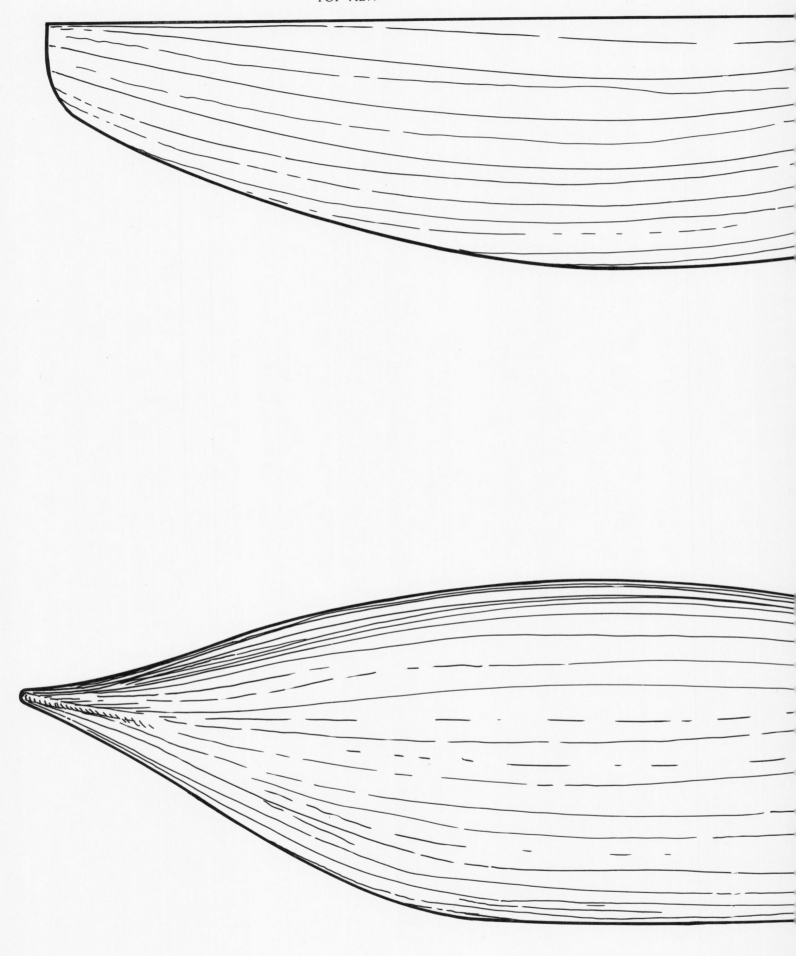

*Plate 3 (left)*

Remove staples to see and use full patterns.

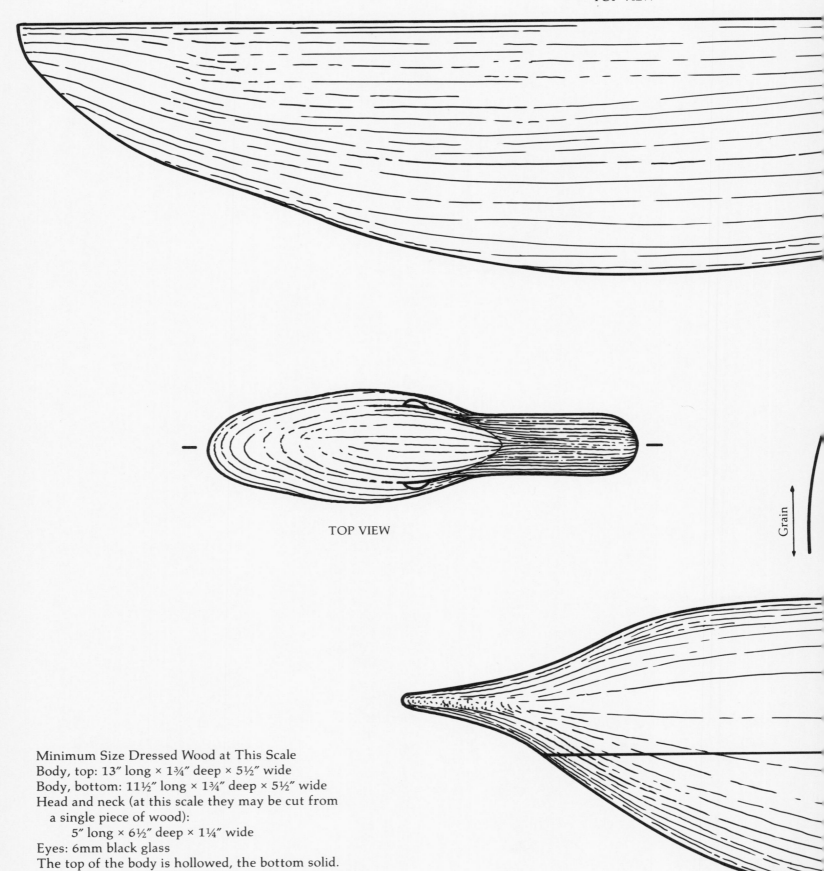

TOP VIEW

Grain

Minimum Size Dressed Wood at This Scale
Body, top: 13" long × 1¾" deep × 5½" wide
Body, bottom: 11½" long × 1¾" deep × 5½" wide
Head and neck (at this scale they may be cut from
   a single piece of wood):
       5" long × 6½" deep × 1¼" wide
Eyes: 6mm black glass
The top of the body is hollowed, the bottom solid.

*Plate 4 (left)*

Remove staples to see and use full patterns.

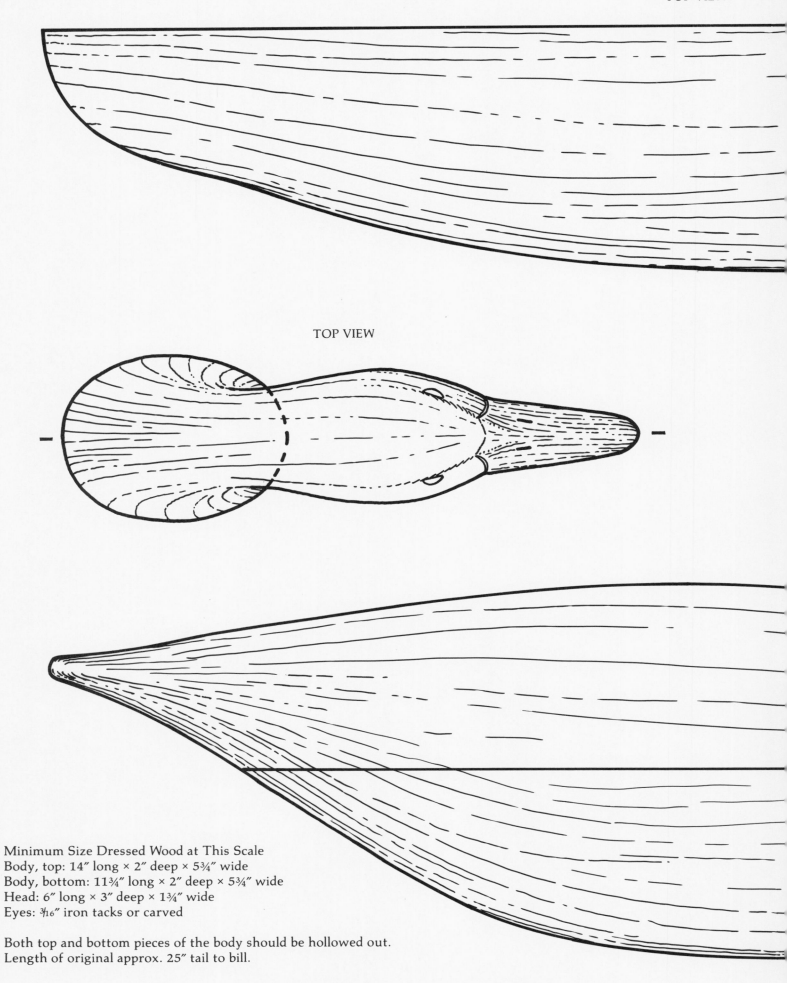

TOP VIEW

Minimum Size Dressed Wood at This Scale
Body, top: 14″ long × 2″ deep × 5¾″ wide
Body, bottom: 11¾″ long × 2″ deep × 5¾″ wide
Head: 6″ long × 3″ deep × 1¾″ wide
Eyes: 3/16″ iron tacks or carved

Both top and bottom pieces of the body should be hollowed out.
Length of original approx. 25″ tail to bill.

*Plate 5 (left)*

Remove staples to see and use full patterns.

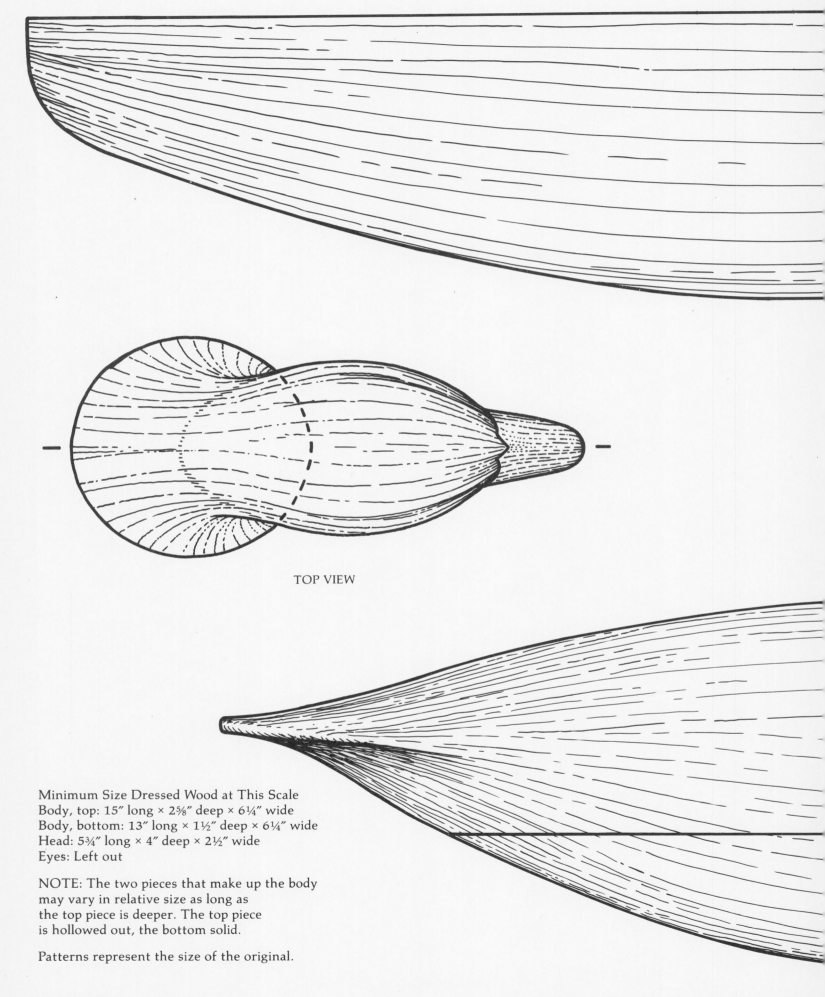

TOP VIEW

Minimum Size Dressed Wood at This Scale
Body, top: 15″ long × 2⅝″ deep × 6¼″ wide
Body, bottom: 13″ long × 1½″ deep × 6¼″ wide
Head: 5¾″ long × 4″ deep × 2½″ wide
Eyes: Left out

NOTE: The two pieces that make up the body
may vary in relative size as long as
the top piece is deeper. The top piece
is hollowed out, the bottom solid.

Patterns represent the size of the original.

*Plate 6 (left)*                    Remove staples to see and use full patterns.

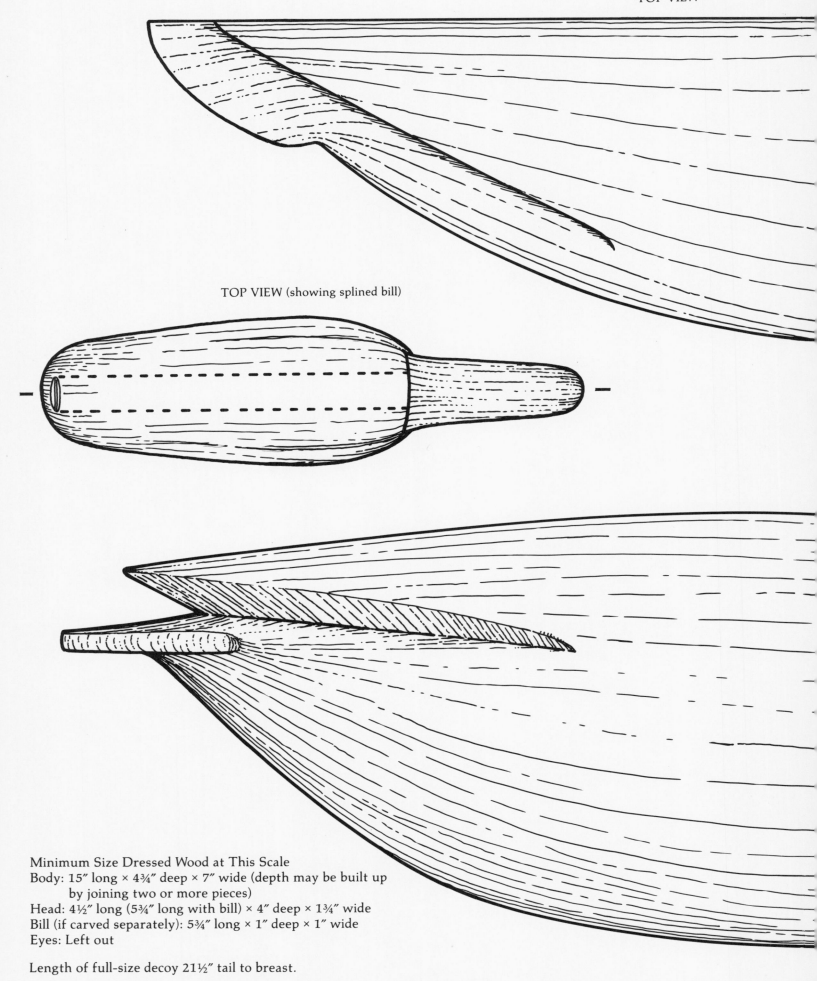

TOP VIEW

TOP VIEW (showing splined bill)

Minimum Size Dressed Wood at This Scale
Body: 15″ long × 4¾″ deep × 7″ wide (depth may be built up
     by joining two or more pieces)
Head: 4½″ long (5¾″ long with bill) × 4″ deep × 1¾″ wide
Bill (if carved separately): 5¾″ long × 1″ deep × 1″ wide
Eyes: Left out

Length of full-size decoy 21½″ tail to breast.

*Plate 7 (left)*

Remove staples to see and use full patterns.

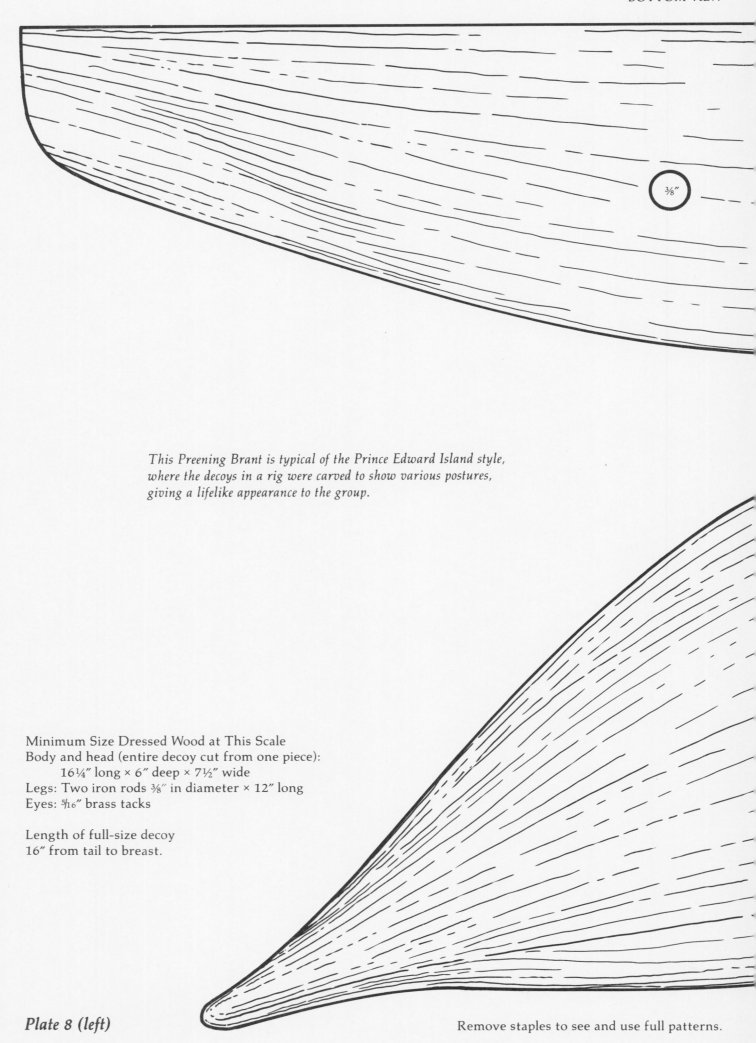

*This Preening Brant is typical of the Prince Edward Island style, where the decoys in a rig were carved to show various postures, giving a lifelike appearance to the group.*

Minimum Size Dressed Wood at This Scale
Body and head (entire decoy cut from one piece):
      16¼″ long × 6″ deep × 7½″ wide
Legs: Two iron rods ⅜″ in diameter × 12″ long
Eyes: ⁵⁄₁₆″ brass tacks

Length of full-size decoy
16″ from tail to breast.

*Plate 8 (left)*

Remove staples to see and use full patterns.

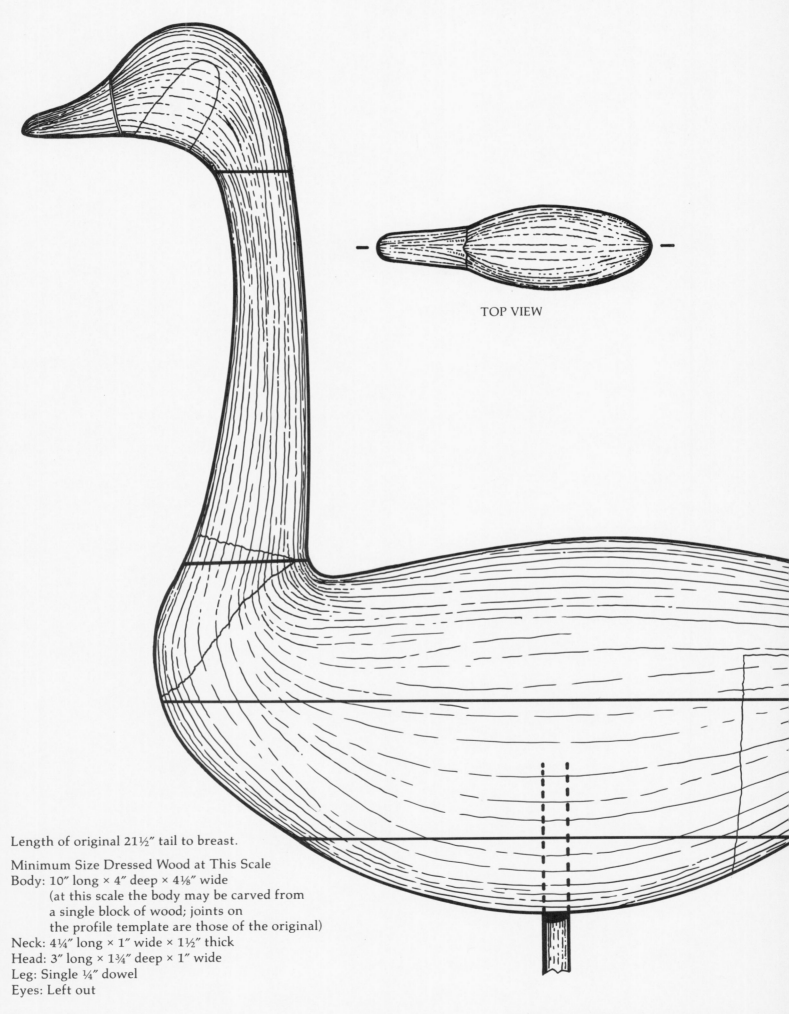

TOP VIEW

Length of original 21½" tail to breast.

Minimum Size Dressed Wood at This Scale
Body: 10" long × 4" deep × 4⅛" wide
        (at this scale the body may be carved from
        a single block of wood; joints on
        the profile template are those of the original)
Neck: 4¼" long × 1" wide × 1½" thick
Head: 3" long × 1¾" deep × 1" wide
Leg: Single ¼" dowel
Eyes: Left out

*Plate 9 (left)*

Remove staples to see and use full patterns.

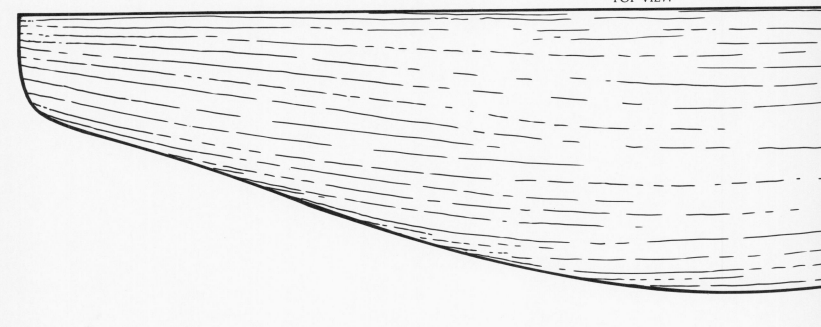

TOP VIEW

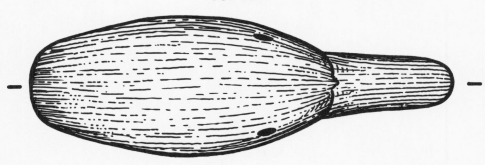

Minimum Size Dressed Wood at This Scale
Body: 15″ long × 4½″ deep × 6¼″ wide
Head and neck: 4½″ long × 5¼″ deep × 1¾″ wide
Eyes: Painted black

Length of original 22″ breast to tail.

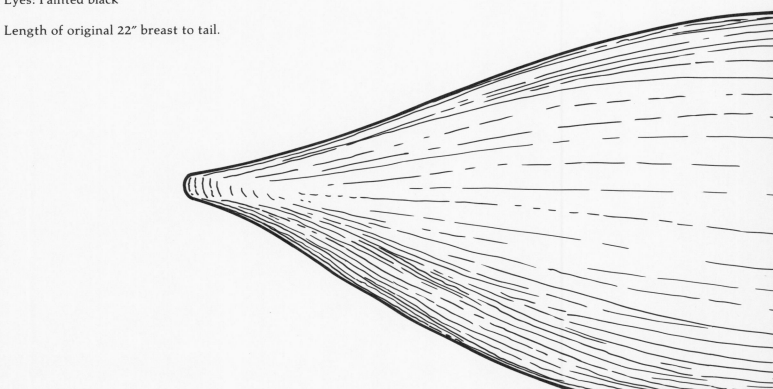

*Plate 10 (left)*

Remove staples to see and use full patterns.

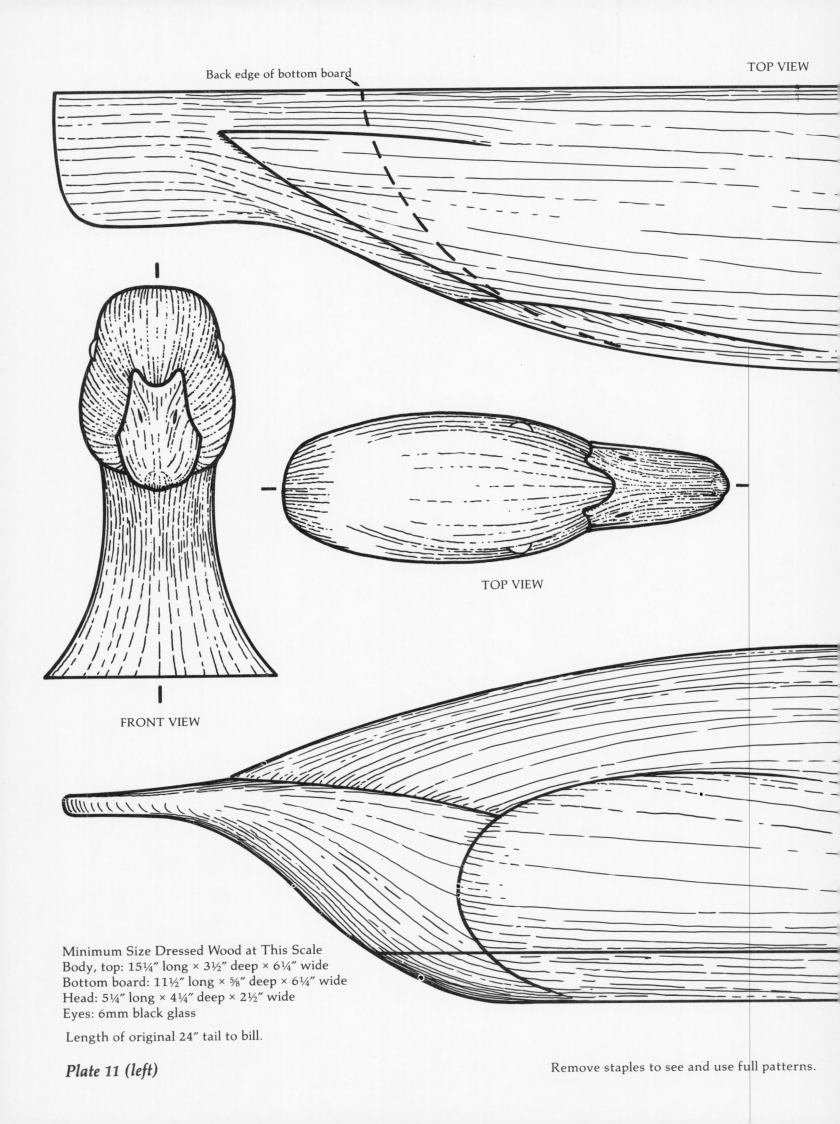

TOP VIEW

Back edge of bottom board

TOP VIEW

FRONT VIEW

Minimum Size Dressed Wood at This Scale
Body, top: 15¼" long × 3½" deep × 6¼" wide
Bottom board: 11½" long × ⅝" deep × 6¼" wide
Head: 5¼" long × 4¼" deep × 2½" wide
Eyes: 6mm black glass

Length of original 24" tail to bill.

*Plate 11 (left)*

Remove staples to see and use full patterns.

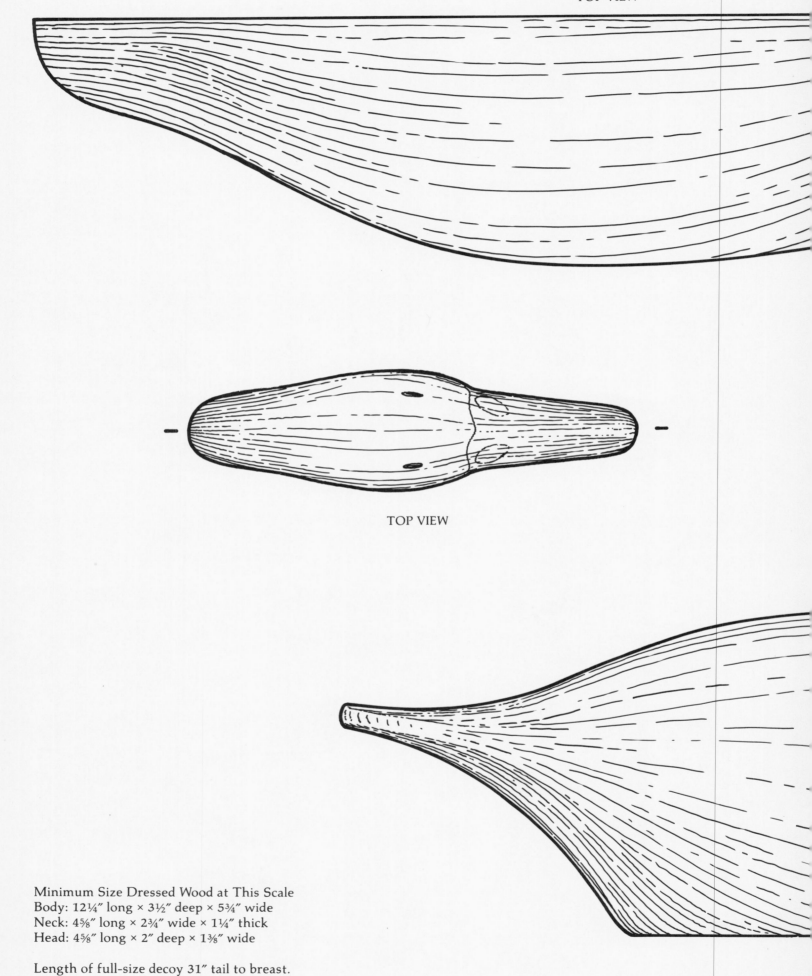

TOP VIEW

Minimum Size Dressed Wood at This Scale
Body: 12¼" long × 3½" deep × 5¾" wide
Neck: 4⅝" long × 2¾" wide × 1¼" thick
Head: 4⅝" long × 2" deep × 1⅜" wide

Length of full-size decoy 31" tail to breast.

*Plate 12 (left)*

Remove staples to see and use full patterns.

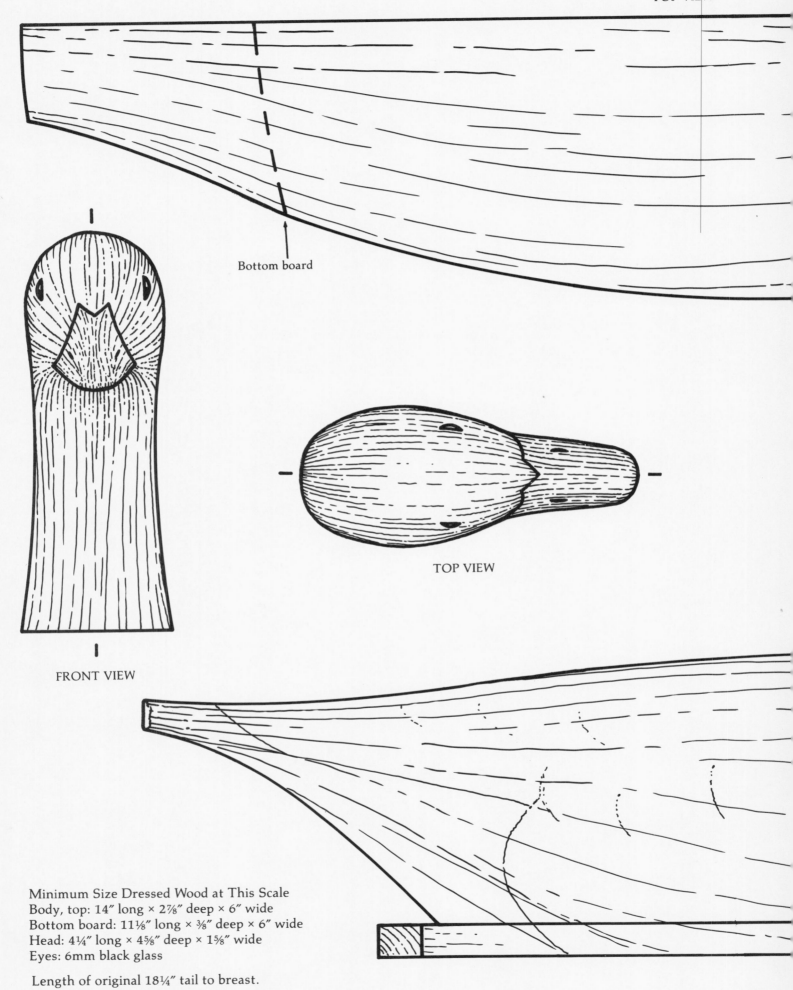

Bottom board

TOP VIEW

FRONT VIEW

Minimum Size Dressed Wood at This Scale
Body, top: 14″ long × 2⅞″ deep × 6″ wide
Bottom board: 11⅛″ long × ⅜″ deep × 6″ wide
Head: 4¼″ long × 4⅝″ deep × 1⅝″ wide
Eyes: 6mm black glass

Length of original 18¼″ tail to breast.

*Plate 13 (left)*

Remove staples to see and use full patterns.

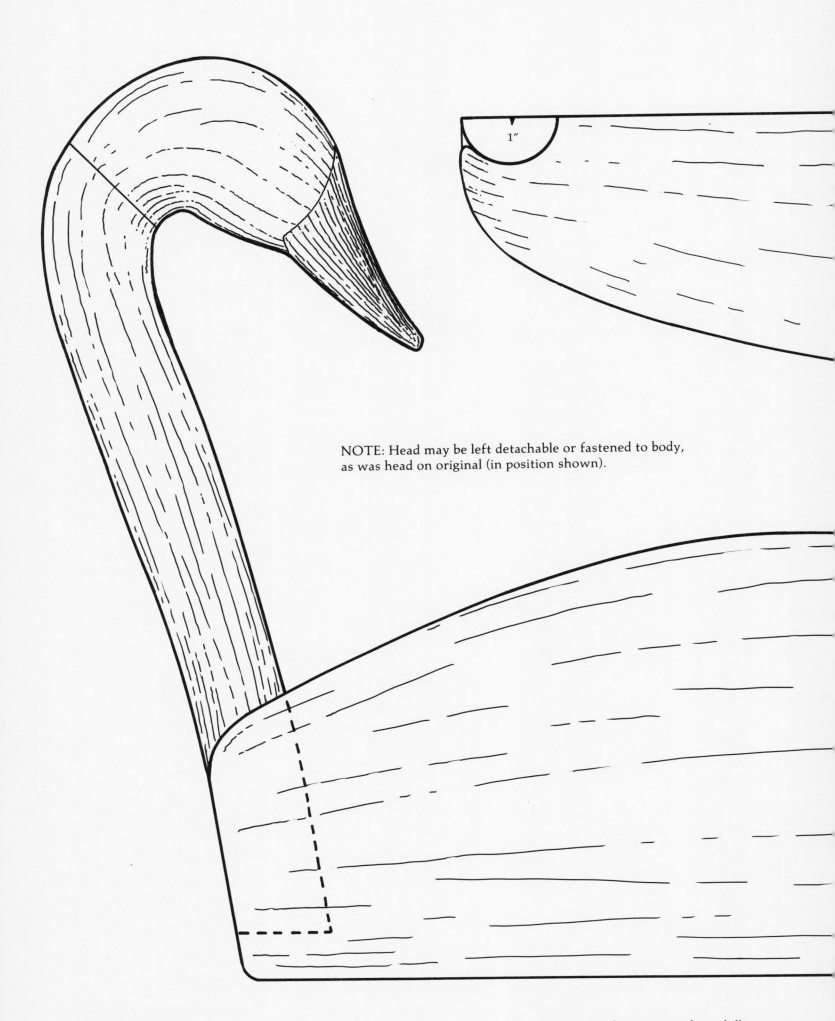

1″

NOTE: Head may be left detachable or fastened to body, as was head on original (in position shown).

*Plate 14 (left)*

Remove staples to see and use full patterns.

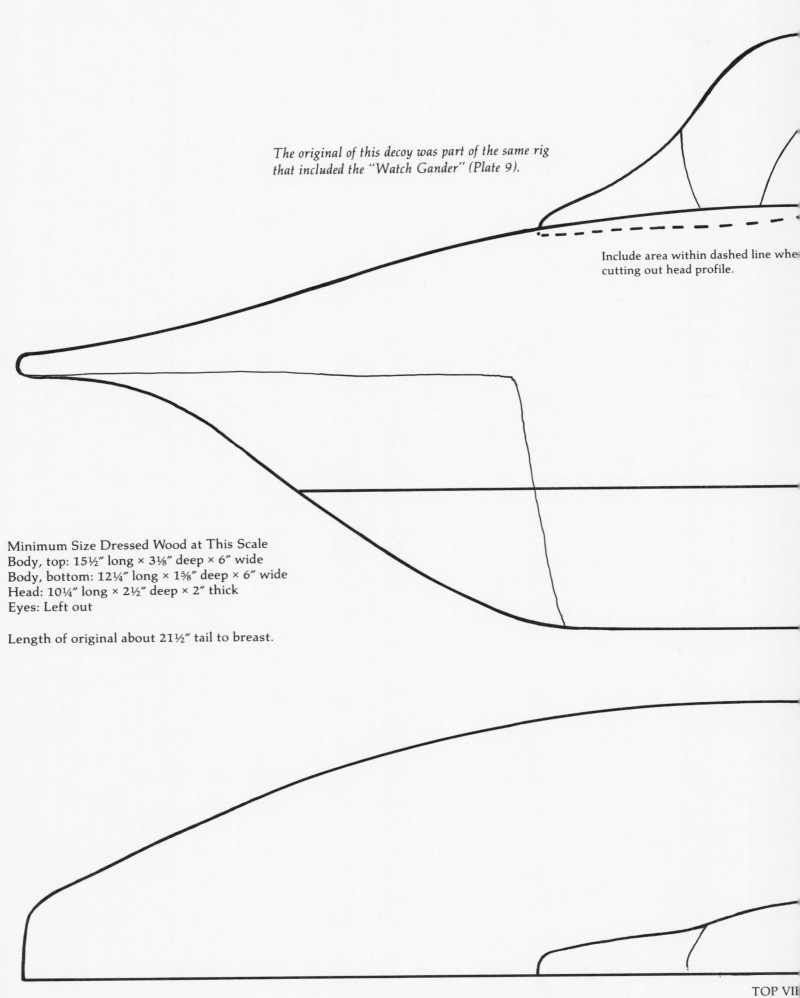

*The original of this decoy was part of the same rig that included the "Watch Gander" (Plate 9).*

Include area within dashed line whe[n] cutting out head profile.

Minimum Size Dressed Wood at This Scale
Body, top: 15½" long × 3⅛" deep × 6" wide
Body, bottom: 12¼" long × 1⅝" deep × 6" wide
Head: 10¼" long × 2½" deep × 2" thick
Eyes: Left out

Length of original about 21½" tail to breast.

*Plate 15 (left)*

Remove staples to see and use full patterns.

TOP VIE[W]

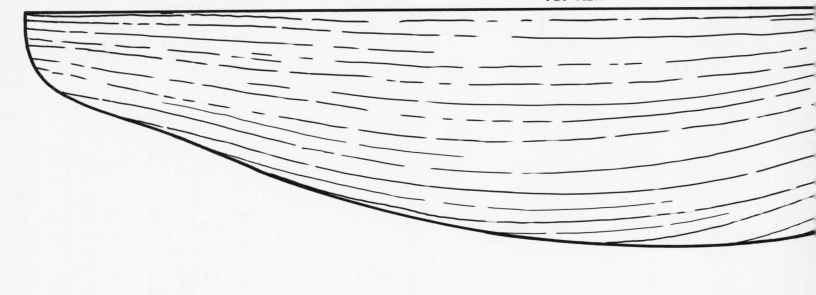

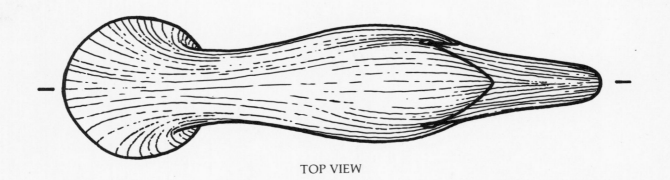

TOP VIEW

Minimum Size Dressed Wood at This Scale
Body, top: 11½″ long × 2½″ deep × 5¼″ wide
Body, bottom: 9″ long × ½″ high × 5½″ wide
Neck: 4″ long × 2½″ thick × 1½″ wide
Head: 4½″ long × 1¾″ deep × 1¼″ wide

Length of original 31″ tail to breast.

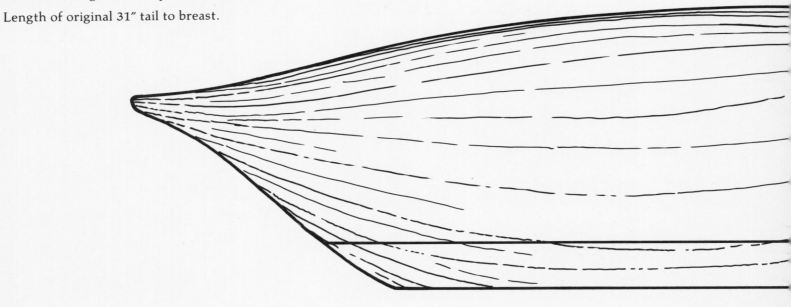

*Plate 16 (left)*

Remove staples to see and use full patterns.

# Whistling Swan

(based on work of unknown carver, Creeds, Va.)

The top of the body is hollowed out, the bottom left solid.

Remove staples to see and use full patterns.

*Plate 16 (right)*

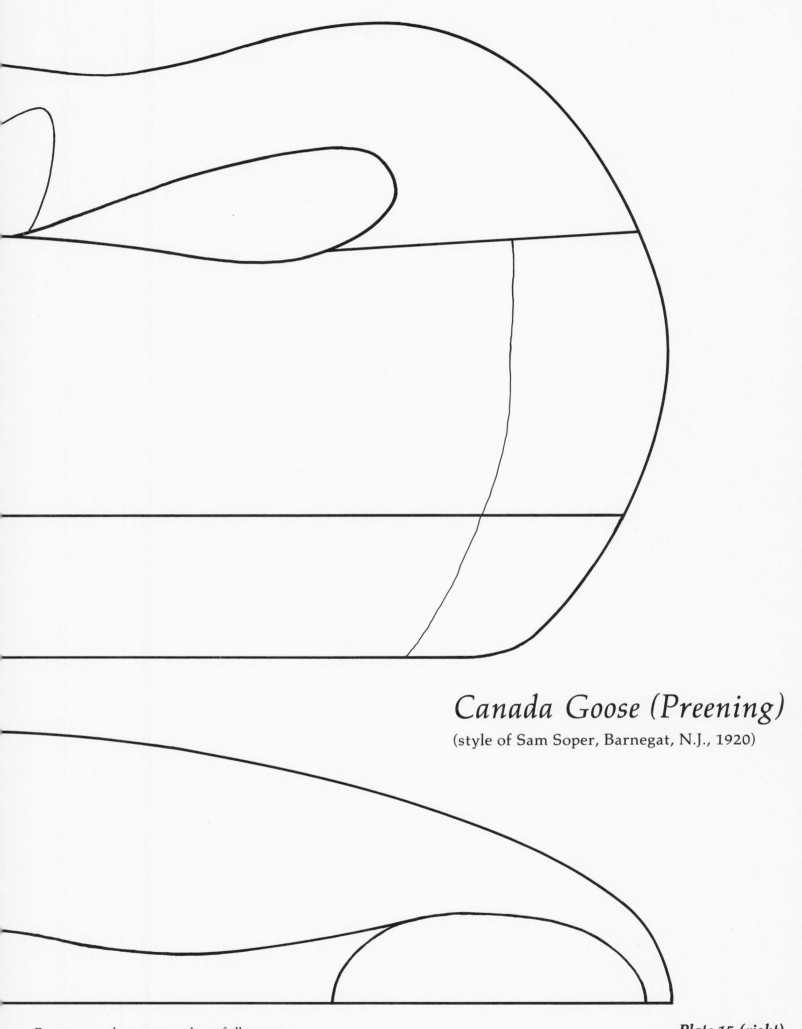

### Canada Goose (Preening)
(style of Sam Soper, Barnegat, N.J., 1920)

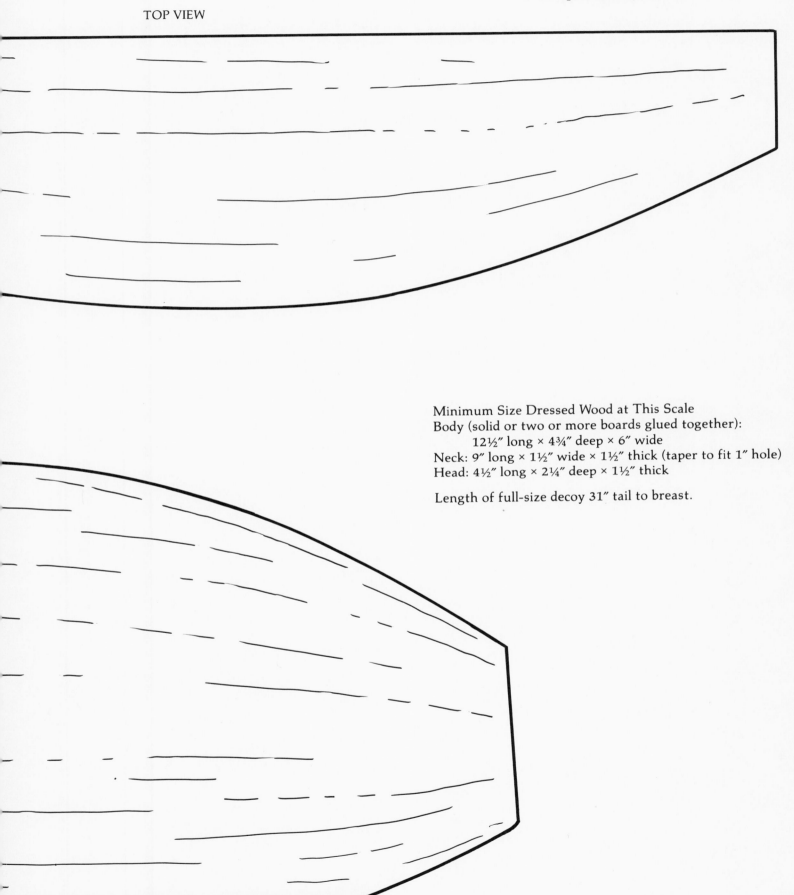

# Whistling Swan
(based on work of unknown carver,
Chesapeake Bay, 1910)

TOP VIEW

Minimum Size Dressed Wood at This Scale
Body (solid or two or more boards glued together):
        12½″ long × 4¾″ deep × 6″ wide
Neck: 9″ long × 1½″ wide × 1½″ thick (taper to fit 1″ hole)
Head: 4½″ long × 2¼″ deep × 1½″ thick

Length of full-size decoy 31″ tail to breast.

Remove staples to see and use full patterns.

*Plate 14 (right)*

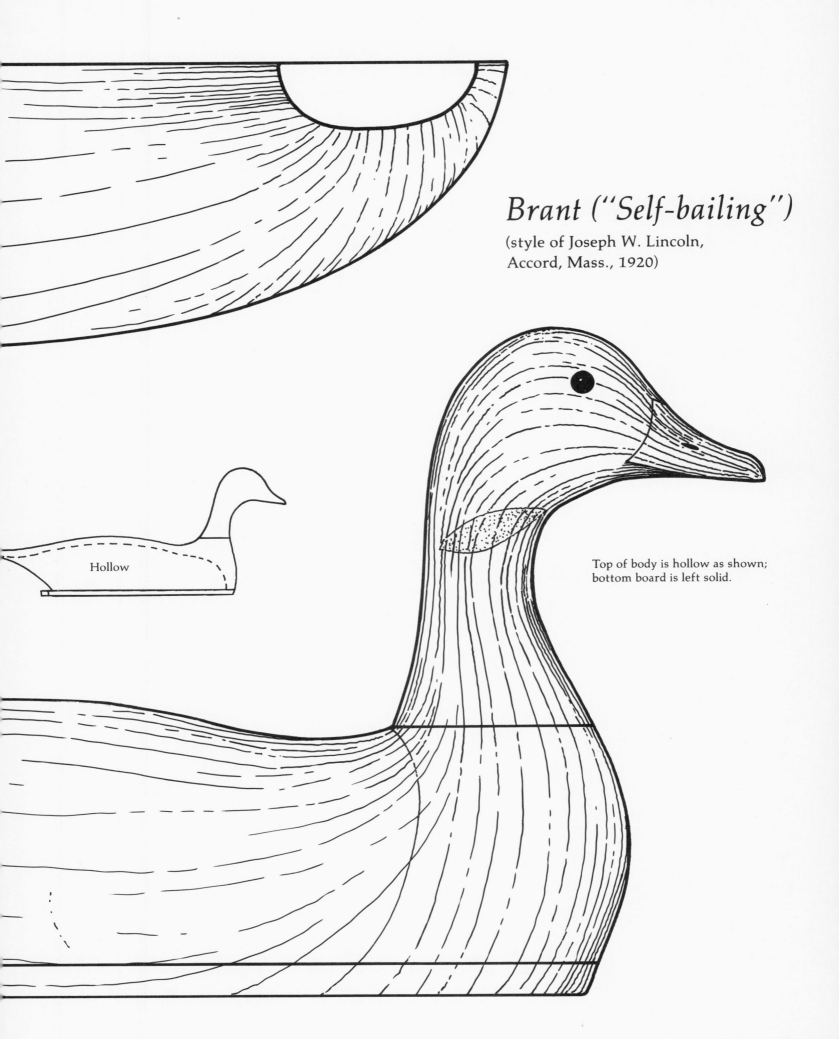

Brant ("Self-bailing")

(style of Joseph W. Lincoln,
Accord, Mass., 1920)

Hollow

Top of body is hollow as shown;
bottom board is left solid.

*Whistling Swan*
(based on work of unknown carver,
Chesapeake Bay)

Remove staples to see and use full patterns.

*Plate 12 (right)*

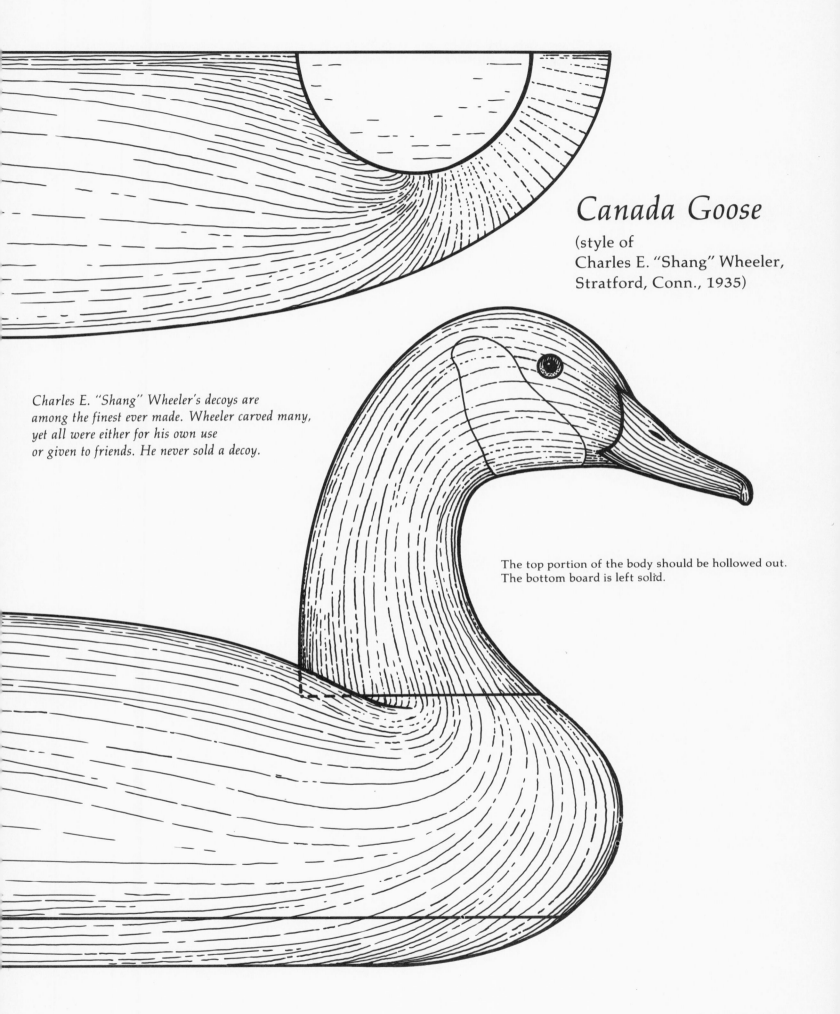

# Canada Goose

(style of
Charles E. "Shang" Wheeler,
Stratford, Conn., 1935)

*Charles E. "Shang" Wheeler's decoys are
among the finest ever made. Wheeler carved many,
yet all were either for his own use
or given to friends. He never sold a decoy.*

The top portion of the body should be hollowed out.
The bottom board is left solid.

Remove staples to see and use full patterns.

*Plate 11 (right)*

Whistling Swan
(style of James Best,
Kitty Hawk, N.C., 1910)

Remove staples to see and use full patterns.

*Plate 10 (right)*

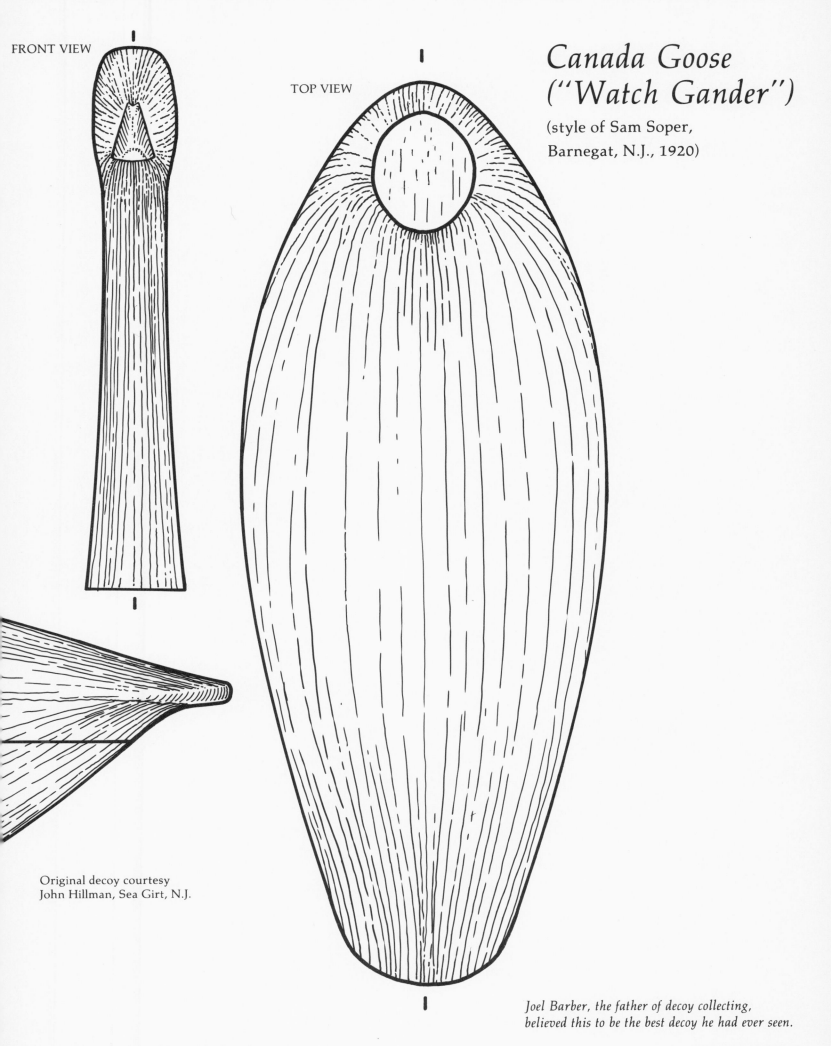

FRONT VIEW

TOP VIEW

*Canada Goose*
*("Watch Gander")*
(style of Sam Soper,
Barnegat, N.J., 1920)

Original decoy courtesy
John Hillman, Sea Girt, N.J.

*Joel Barber, the father of decoy collecting,*
*believed this to be the best decoy he had ever seen.*

**Plate 9 (right)**

Remove staples to see and use full patterns.

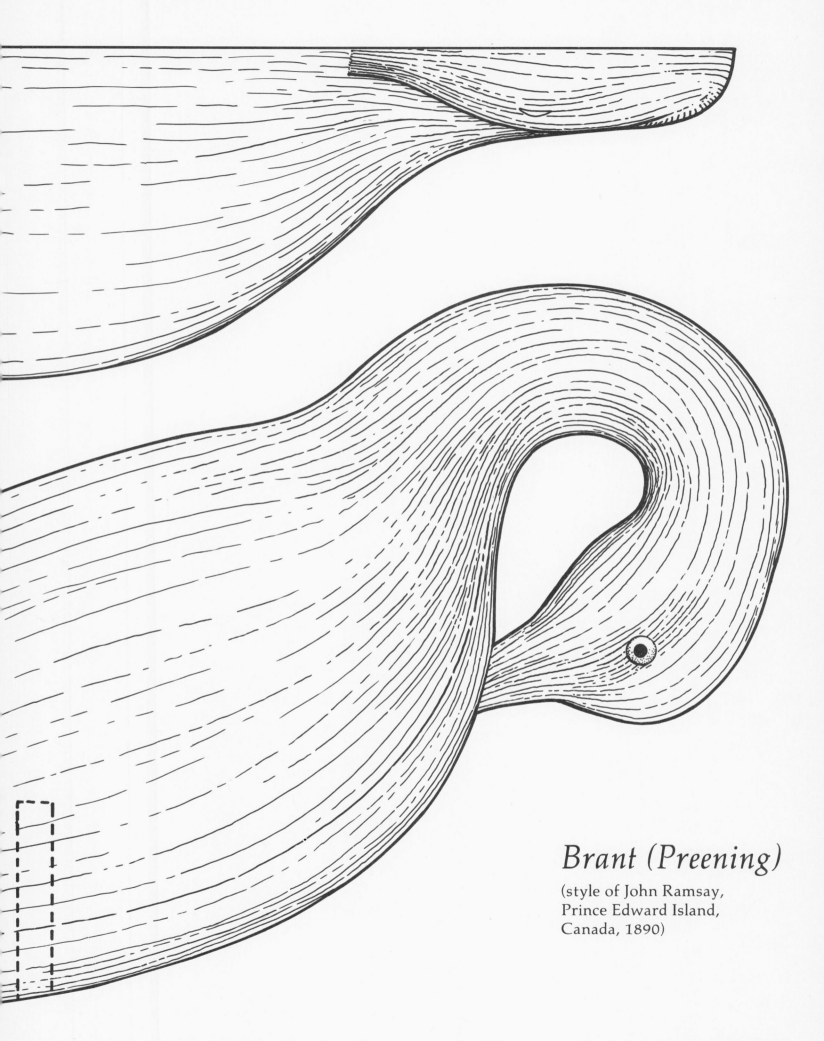

*Brant (Preening)*

(style of John Ramsay,
Prince Edward Island,
Canada, 1890)

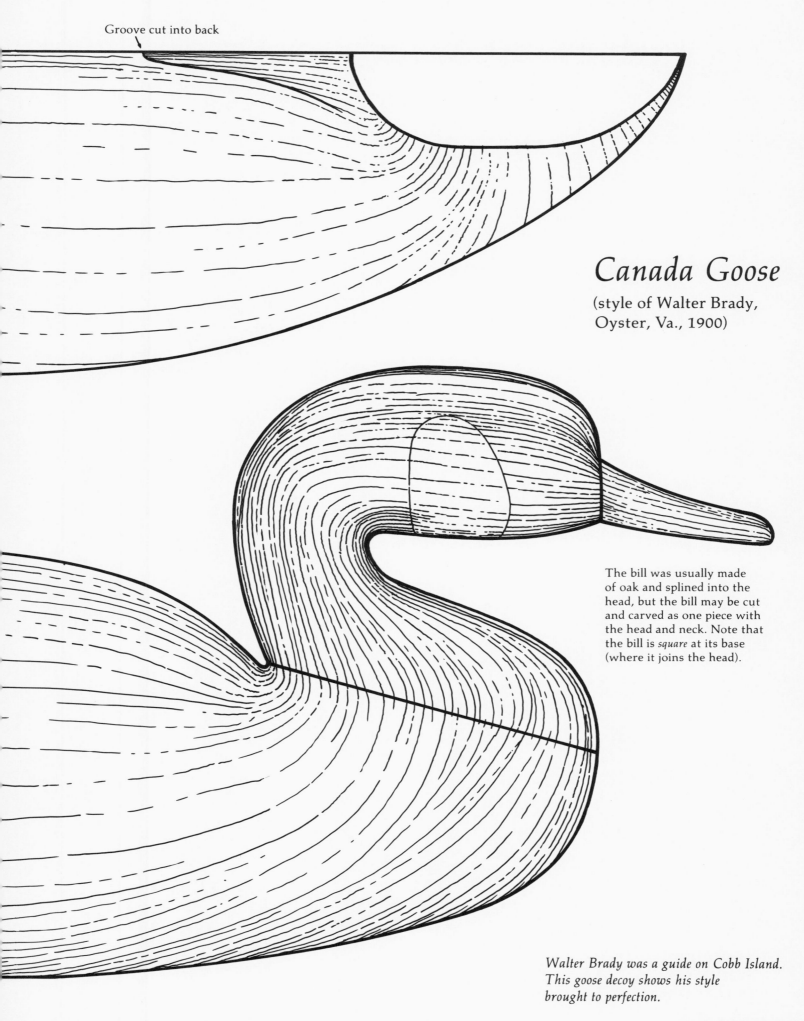

Groove cut into back

# Canada Goose

(style of Walter Brady,
Oyster, Va., 1900)

The bill was usually made
of oak and splined into the
head, but the bill may be cut
and carved as one piece with
the head and neck. Note that
the bill is *square* at its base
(where it joins the head).

*Walter Brady was a guide on Cobb Island.*
*This goose decoy shows his style*
*brought to perfection.*

Remove staples to see and use full patterns.

**Plate 7 (right)**

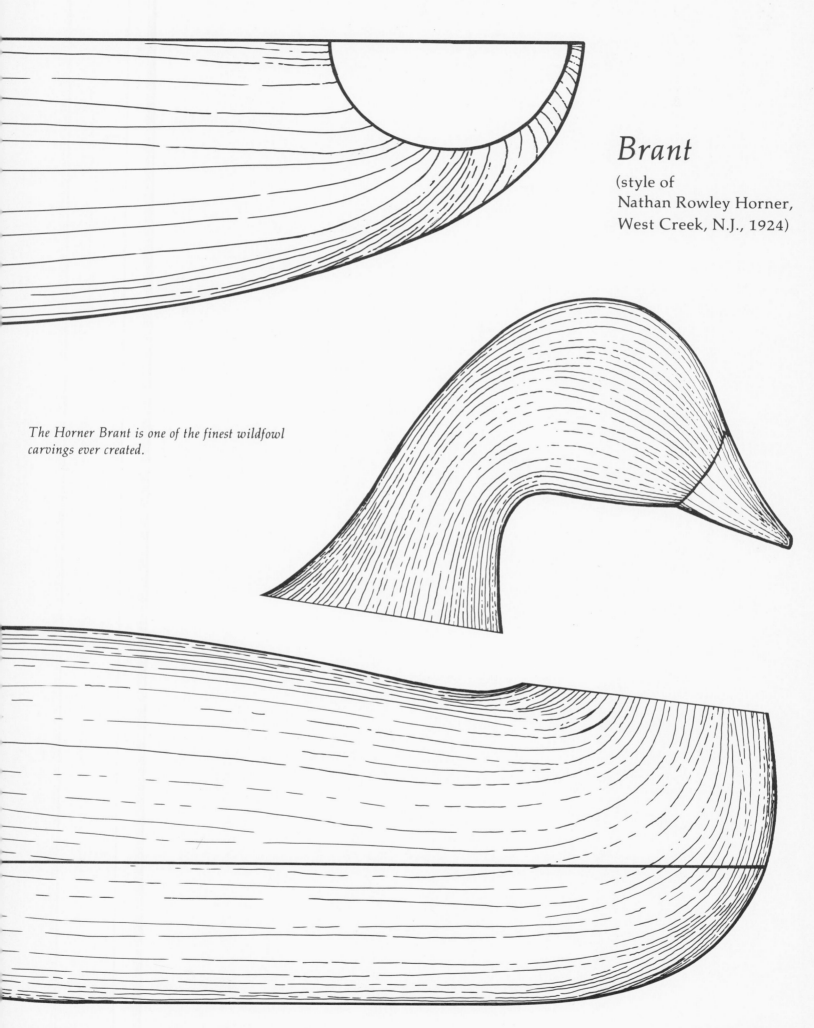

# Brant

(style of
Nathan Rowley Horner,
West Creek, N.J., 1924)

*The Horner Brant is one of the finest wildfowl carvings ever created.*

Remove staples to see and use full patterns.

*Plate 6 (right)*

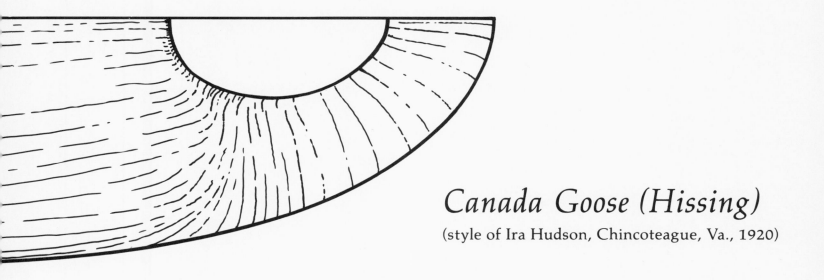

# Canada Goose (Hissing)
(style of Ira Hudson, Chincoteague, Va., 1920)

*Plate 5 (right)*

# Whistling Swan
### (style of Charles Birch, Willis Wharf, Va., 1930)

Grain

edge

Joint

Grain

Splined Oak Bill

Joints used by Charles Birch
in full-size decoy

Remove staples to see and use full patterns.

*Plate 4 (right)*

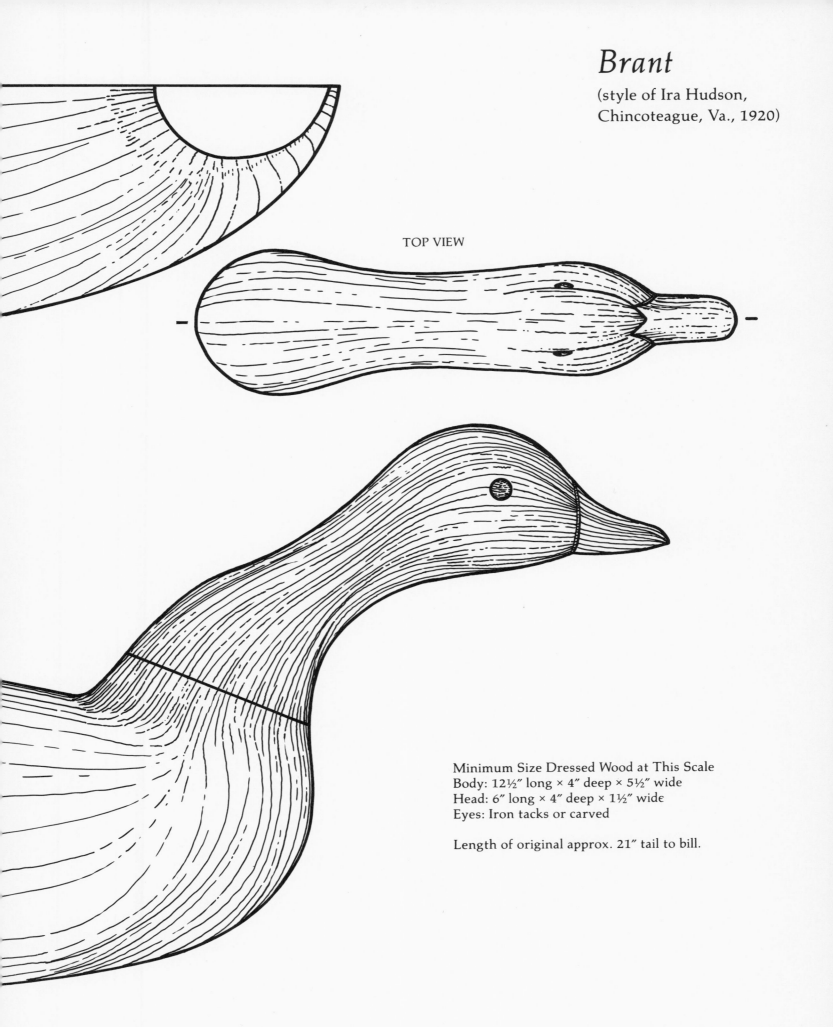

# Brant

(style of Ira Hudson,
Chincoteague, Va., 1920)

TOP VIEW

Minimum Size Dressed Wood at This Scale
Body: 12½" long × 4" deep × 5½" wide
Head: 6" long × 4" deep × 1½" wide
Eyes: Iron tacks or carved

Length of original approx. 21" tail to bill.

Remove staples to see and use full patterns.

*Plate 3 (right)*

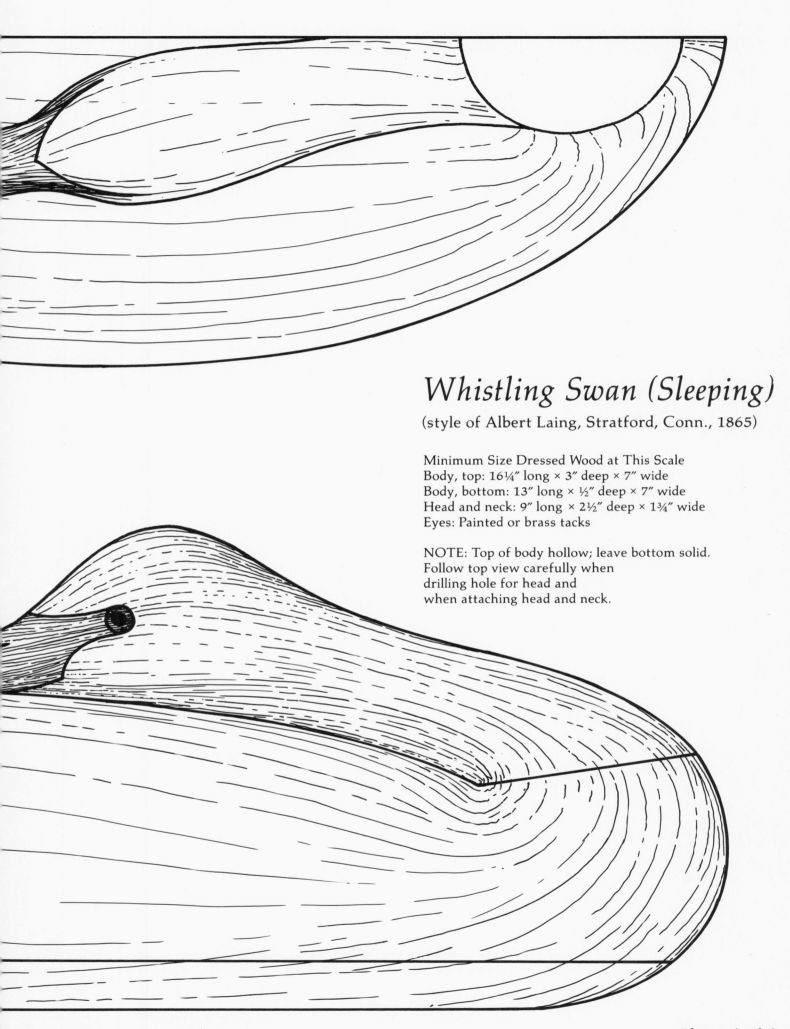

# Whistling Swan (Sleeping)

(style of Albert Laing, Stratford, Conn., 1865)

Minimum Size Dressed Wood at This Scale
Body, top: 16¼" long × 3" deep × 7" wide
Body, bottom: 13" long × ½" deep × 7" wide
Head and neck: 9" long × 2½" deep × 1¾" wide
Eyes: Painted or brass tacks

NOTE: Top of body hollow; leave bottom solid.
Follow top view carefully when
drilling hole for head and
when attaching head and neck.

# Whistling Swan

(style of James or William Holly,
Havre de Grace, Md., 1890)

Grain

Minimum Size Dressed Wood at This Scale
Body: 12″ long × 3¾″ deep × 5″ wide
Head: 6″ long × 5¾″ deep × 1¼″ wide
Eyes: Brass tacks (may be simulated with
¼″ dowels rounded at end)

Remove staples to see and use full patterns.

***Plate 1 (right)***

even those intended only for decorative purposes will be stabler this way.

Now assemble the two halves, using a good water-proof glue, and toenail using 3DD galvanized finishing nails, nailing the bottom to the top (Fig. 4). Further smooth and fair the body with a spokeshave or rasp (Fig. 5).

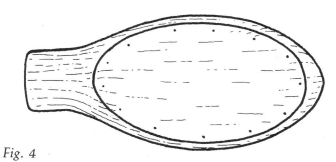

Fig. 4

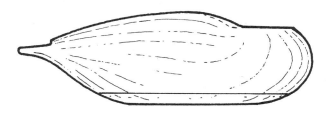

Fig. 5

Fig. 6

Look at the head from the top. Make sure that the cross-section line remains clearly marked. Using the profile pattern as a guide, mark a line across the upper side of the bill, perpendicular to the cross-section line, indicating where the top of the bill ends (Fig. 8). Mark another line across where the underside of the bill ends, corresponding to the line just made above, also perpendicular to the cross-section line. Generally, bill width can be determined by marking guidelines along the bill at a point halfway between the center line and the outside edge. Do this on each side of the cross-section line (Fig. 8).

## The Head

The head of your decoy will demand more time and effort than the body. Generally, what you want to achieve in your carving, especially of the head, is symmetry of form. In other words, the eyes should be opposite each other! Also, both cheeks should be equally puffy, and the neck and top of the head should have the same graceful curves on either side. Many superdetailed decorative carvings are spoiled simply because of unevenness in the basic carving.

Using a piece of pine or other suitable wood of the specified dimensions, lay the head profile pattern so that the grain of the wood runs *with the bill*. Make sure the base of the neck is even with the bottom edge of the wood. Cut out on a band saw. After sawing out the head shape, measure the half-thickness of your stock. With a pencil, mark down the middle of the entire head block on all sawn surfaces. *Never cut this line away!* It is the cross section of the head and should be there when you finish-sand your carving.

At this point you may want to drill guide holes for the eyes, while the sides of the head are flat. Use a drill press if available (Fig. 6).

Next, taper the sides of the head from top to bottom. Whittle this taper with a knife. Keep checking both sides (Fig. 7).

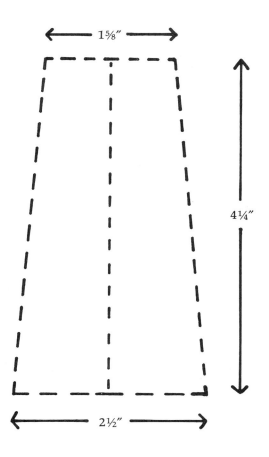

← 1⅝" →

4¼"

← 2½" →

Fig. 7

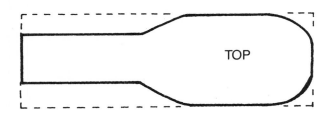

Fig. 8

Fig. 9

Bill width can now be achieved by sawing or carving to these guidelines, making sure that both sides of the bill are symmetrical in relation to the cross-section line (Fig. 9). Whether you carve the bill first or last is a matter of personal preference. You can mark the cuts for bill width and then start at the neck.

Carve off the corners of the neck and make it nice and round. Carve into the eye area and make a nice full cheek and round off the top of the head (Fig. 10). Cut in the bill where it joins the "face." (On one decoy, Plate 4, the original carver used a "splined" bill. Follow the diagram on the plate to determine how to do this, if you wish to duplicate the original precisely. More information on splining is given in my book *Carving*

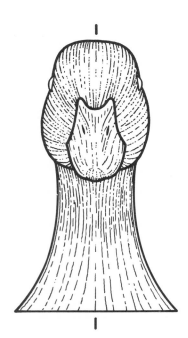

Fig. 10

Fig. 11

*Classical Regional Shorebirds,* Dover 25072-5.) If the head pattern indicates additional details such as nostrils, add them now. Do not be surprised if your decoy lacks these details, however; many "working" decoys had very few or no details. Next fit the head to the body, using a block plane if necessary to get a nice fit. Glue and toenail the head in place, using 1" brads (Fig. 11).

## Completing the Carving

Sand the assembled decoy smooth and add the eyes. If called for, paint the eyes on, and with a drop of varnish or clear nail polish on them they will really look good. Or the model may call for glass eyes. These are put in by drilling a hole the size of the eye (a 5/16" bit for 8mm eyes), filling with plastic wood, and pushing in the eye. Wipe off plastic wood that squeezes out (Fig. 11).

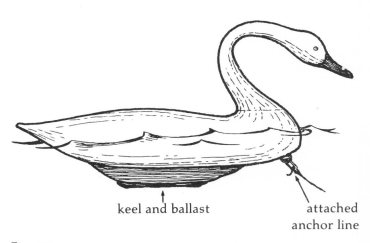

keel and ballast          attached
                          anchor line

Fig. 12

At this point I should mention that all of the decoys here were originally ballasted by strips or pads of lead. On most of the swans, these were attached to wooden keels which were in turn attached to the bottom of the decoys—a necessary arrangement to assure the upright position in the water of such bulky decoys (see Fig. 12). It was equally necessary, however, to remove the keel and ballast if the decoy was being used as a decoration or became part of somebody's collection. Such paraphernalia, necessary in the water, made for a lopsided display on land! Often, even so, a staple may be found remaining attached to the breast on these old decoys; this, or a similar thong or loop, was for the attachment of an anchor line (Fig. 12).

## Finishing Your Antique Decoy

Decoys may be finished in different ways. There is space here to offer only a few pointers on finishing. Just remember that the old-time decoy carvers were less concerned with painting in realistic detail than many carvers of today. To aid you in imitating the styles of the originators of the decoys in this collection, color photographs of each appear on the covers. Study these carefully. If you prefer, any of these decoys may be given a natural finish rather than painted. This has the effect of bringing out the grain of the wood. For a natural finish, go over the wood again with #220 sandpaper to create an extremely smooth surface. Make sure you have sanded out all blemishes. If you desire, you may stain the wood a different color at this point; allow to dry thoroughly. Finally, apply a coat of varnish or shellac, following the directions on the can.

Generally, traditional decoys were painted, and you will probably want to paint yours. There are as many ways of painting decoys as there are decoy carvers. I can offer here just a few basic tips and procedures. First, it is necessary to seal and prime the wood to fill the pores and provide a suitable base to paint over. Sealer and primer may be purchased in any paint store. I particularly recommend "Kilz" primer-sealer, an excellent product of Masterchem Industries. This saves you a step by priming and sealing in one operation; best of all, "Kilz" can be covered with either oils or acrylics. (When using acrylics, however, it is a good idea to top the "Kilz" with a coat of an acrylic primer to insure maximum adhesion of the final coat of paint.) Primers are usually white, but they can be tinted if you desire.

After applying primer, let dry the required time, and then sand with #220 sandpaper to provide a smooth surface for painting. The question of whether to use oil or acrylic paint must be faced. Acrylics are more popular and are recommended for the beginner because they dry quickly and allow brushes to be cleaned with soap and water. Just remember to use an oil-base primer under oil paint, and an acrylic primer under acrylic paint.

When painting decoys, apply large, basic areas of color first. If you let the paint dry, you can then use a dry-brush technique to stipple on feathers. If you wish colors to blend into each other with no discernible edge, use a wet-on-wet technique. Again, study the color photographs on the covers. Some traditional decoy carvers combined paint with a natural finish. You may wish to experiment with different methods.

You may also want to make your goose or swan look like a genuine antique. There are various methods of simulating age and wear. For a minimal appearance of aging, you can apply "Min-Wax Special Dark Walnut" paste wax. A method of simulating natural wear and tear is to sand off some of the finish. More extreme methods include simulating shot holes and judiciously beating the hell out of the carving. Inventive minds will no doubt improve on this aspect of finishing the decoy.

A final word of advice. *Sign and date your work!* I cannot stress this too strongly. Some people who have created convincing replicas of antiques might be led into temptation. Don't be one of them! I can think of no easier way of damaging your reputation than trying to pass off forgeries on unsuspecting collectors. Losing the trust of those you deal with will never be worth any temporary gain.